The Ivy Lee Method The Daily Routine Experts Recommend for Peak Productivity

Author

Sikandar Sami

Contents

The Ivy Lee Method 3

What makes it so compelling? 4

On Managing Priorities Well 5

This is what makes it so compelling: 5

Profitability, Simplified 6

Sounds basic. Nobody does it. 6

Why It Works 7

Why We Don't Do It 8

Not a Morning Person? 8

No concerns, evening people. 9

I discover morning to work best. Your mileage may shift. 9

1. Decide what you need to be acceptable at doing. 10

2. Ask somebody who has been there. 11

3. Get the fundamental thought, avoid the subtleties. 11

We should all take a full breath. 12

This is what they resembled... 12

4. Go moderate. 13

5. Try not to miss exercises. 14

Unendingly. 15

6. Pick an activity and begin 15

Pick one that you might want to be acceptable at and begin. 16

How I Met Sir Richard Branson 18

The Habits of Successful People 19

    This is what I think has a significant effect: 19

    Start Now 19

The Dangerous Mistake We All Make 22

How regularly do you do this in your own life? 23

Clearness Leads to Direction 23

Start It Now 24

The Ivy Lee Method: The Daily Routine Experts Recommend for Peak Productivity

By 1918, Charles M. Schwab was probably the most extravagant man on the planet.

Schwab was the leader of the Bethlehem Steel Corporation, the biggest shipbuilder and the second-biggest steel maker in America at that point. The renowned creator Thomas Edison once alluded to Schwab as the "ace trickster." He was continually looking for an edge over the opposition.

One day in 1918, in his journey to expand the effectiveness of his group and find better approaches to complete things, Schwab organized a gathering with an exceptionally regarded efficiency advisor named Ivy Lee.

Lee was a fruitful money manager in his own privilege and is broadly recognized as a pioneer in the field of advertising. Supposedly, Schwab brought Lee into his office and stated, "Show me an approach to complete more things."

"Allow me 15 minutes with every one of your heads," Lee answered.

"How much will it cost me," Schwab inquired.

"Nothing," Lee said. "Except if it works. Following three months, you can send me a check for whatever you feel it's worth to you."

Book: The Ivy Lee Method The Daily Routine Experts Recommend for Peak Productivity
Author: Sikandar Sami

The Ivy Lee Method

During his 15 minutes with every chief, Ivy Lee clarified his straightforward day by day schedule for accomplishing top profitability:

Toward the finish of each work day, record the six most significant things you have to achieve tomorrow. Try not to record in excess of six assignments.

Organize those six things arranged by their actual significance.

At the point when you show up tomorrow, focus just on the main assignment. Work until the main errand is done before proceeding onward to the subsequent undertaking.

Approach the remainder of your rundown in a similar manner. Toward the day's end, move any incomplete things to another rundown of six errands for the next day.

Rehash this cycle each working day.

The methodology sounded basic, yet Schwab and his leader group at Bethlehem Steel checked it out. Following three months, Schwab was so pleased with the advancement his organization had made that he called Lee into his office and thought of him a check for $25,000.

A $25,000 check written in 1918 is what could be compared to a $400,000 check in 2015.

The Ivy Lee Method of organizing your plan for the day appears to be moronically basic. How could something this straightforward be worth to such an extent?

What makes it so compelling?

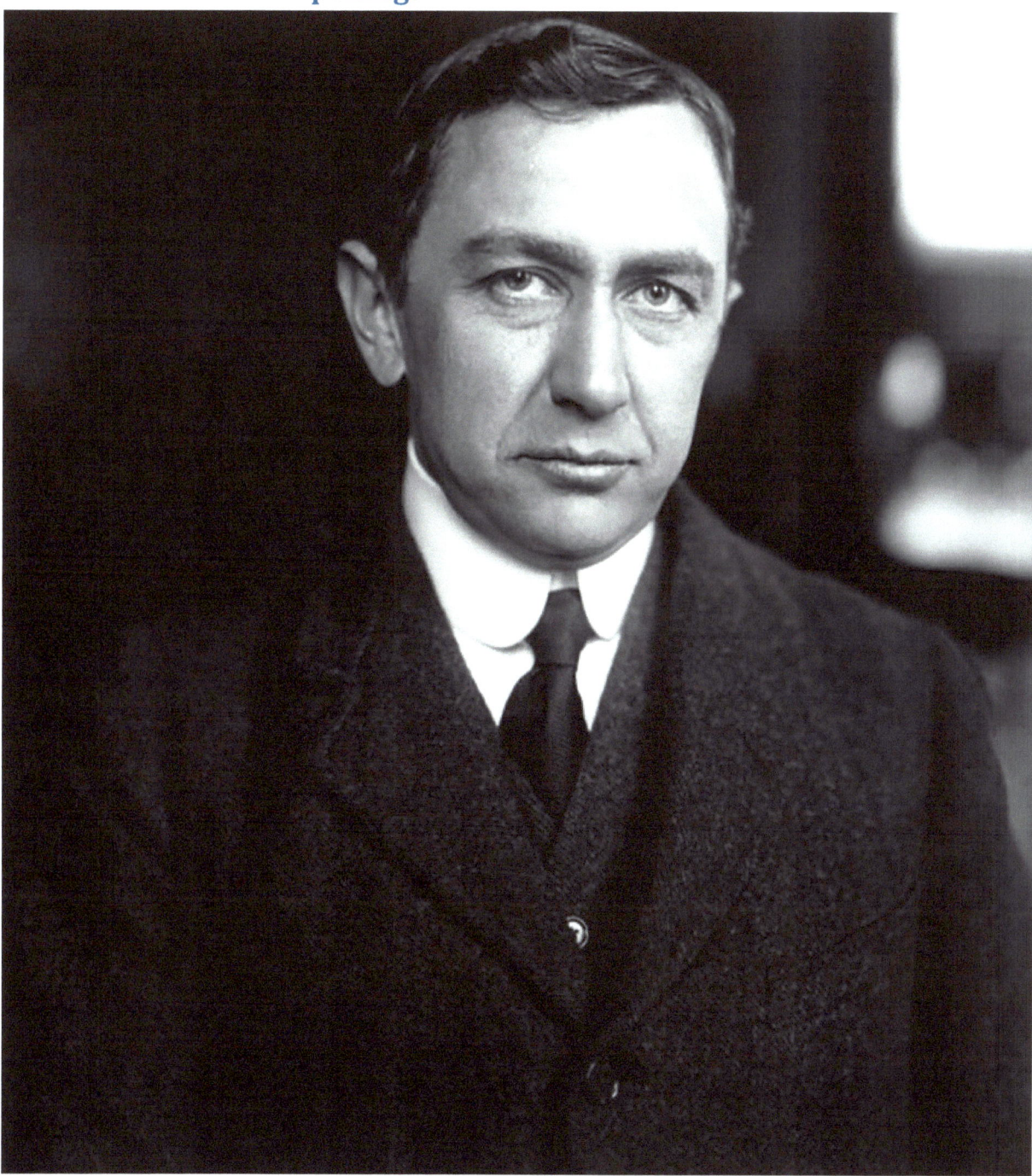

On Managing Priorities Well

Ivy Lee's profitability technique uses a large number of the ideas I have expounded on already.

This is what makes it so compelling:

It's straightforward enough to really work. The essential evaluate of strategies like this one is that they are excessively fundamental. They don't represent the entirety of the complexities and subtleties of life. What occurs if a crisis springs up? Shouldn't something be said about utilizing the most recent innovation for our fullest potential benefit? As far as I can tell, unpredictability is frequently a shortcoming since it makes it harder to refocus. Truly, crises and sudden interruptions will emerge. Overlook them however much as could reasonably be expected, manage them when you should, and return to your organized plan for the day at the earliest opportunity. Utilize straightforward principles to control complex conduct.

It compels you to settle on extreme choices. I don't accept there is anything mystical about Lee's number of six significant assignments for every day. It could simply be five undertakings for every day. Nonetheless, I do think there is something mysterious about overwhelming cutoff points upon yourself. I find that the absolute best activity when you have such a large number of thoughts (or when you're overpowered by all that you have to complete) is to prune your thoughts and trim away all that isn't totally fundamental. Requirements can improve you. Lee's technique is like Warren Buffett's 25-5 Rule, which expects you to concentrate on only 5 basic errands and overlook everything else. Essentially, in the event that you focus on nothing, you'll be occupied by everything.

It eliminates the contact of beginning. The greatest obstacle to completing most errands is beginning them. (Getting off the lounge chair can be intense, however once you really begin running it is a lot simpler to complete your exercise.) Lee's strategy compels you to choose your first errand the prior night you go to work. This system has been fantastically helpful for me: as an essayist, I can squander three or four hours discussing what I ought to expound on a given day. On the off chance that I choose the prior night, nonetheless, I can wake up and begin composing right away. It's basic, yet it works. First and foremost, beginning is similarly as significant as prevailing by any means.

Book: The Ivy Lee Method The Daily Routine Experts Recommend for Peak Productivity
Author: Sikandar Sami

It expects you to single-task. Present day society adores performing various tasks. The legend of performing multiple tasks is that being occupied is inseparable from being better. The specific inverse is valid. Having less needs prompts better work. Study a-list specialists in almost any field—competitors, craftsmen, researchers, educators, CEOs—and you'll find one trademark goes through every one of them: center. The explanation is straightforward. You can't be incredible at one assignment in case you're continually separating your time ten distinct ways. Authority requires center and consistency.

The primary concern? Do the most significant thing first every day. It's the main profitability stunt you need.

The Only Productivity Tip You'll Ever Need

Ernest Hemingway woke every morning and started composing straight away.

He portrayed his day by day schedule by saying, "When I am chipping away at a book or a story I compose each morning as not long after first light as could be expected under the circumstances. There is nobody to upset you and it is cool or cold and you go to your work and warm as you compose."

Profitability, Simplified

No compelling reason to coax this out. This profitability tip is direct: Do the most significant thing first every day.

Sounds basic. Nobody does it.

Much the same as Hemingway, who delivered an amazing volume of high-bore work during his vocation, you can gain astounding ground every day in the event that you basically do the most significant thing first.

Why It Works

We regularly expect that efficiency implies completing more things every day. Wrong. Efficiency is completing significant things reliably. What's more, regardless of what you are really going after, there are just a couple of things that are genuinely significant.

Being beneficial is tied in with keeping up a consistent, normal speed on a couple of things, not greatest speed on everything.

That is the reason this methodology is powerful. In the event that you do the most significant thing first every day, at that point you'll generally complete something significant. I don't think about you, however this is a serious deal for me. There are numerous days when I squander hours check off the fourth, fifth, or sixth most significant errands on my plan for the day and never get around to doing the most significant thing.

As you'll see underneath, there is no explanation you need to apply this technique toward the beginning of the day, however I figure beginning your day with the most significant undertaking offers some extra advantages over different occasions.

To start with, self discipline will in general be higher prior in the day. That implies you'll have the option to give your best vitality and exertion to your most significant assignment.

Second, in my experience, the more profound I get into the day, the almost certain it is that sudden assignments will crawl into my timetable and the more outlandish it is that I'll invest my energy as I had arranged. Doing the most significant thing first every day evades that.

At long last, the human brain appears to loathe incomplete activities. They make an uncertain strain and inner pressure. At the point when we begin something, we need to complete it. You are bound to complete an undertaking subsequent to beginning it, so start the significant assignments as quickly as time permits. (Simply one more motivation behind why beginning is a higher priority than succeeding.)

Why We Don't Do It

The vast majority invest the greater part of their energy reacting to another person's plan than their own.

I think this is somewhat an aftereffect of how we are raised by society. In school, we are given tasks and advised when to step through our exams. At work, we are relegated due dates and given desires from our bosses. At home, we have undertakings or tasks to perform to think about our children and our accomplices. Following a couple of many years of this, it can turn out to be anything but difficult to go through your day responding to the boosts that encompass you. We figure out how to make a move as a response to the desires, requests, or needs of another person.

So normally, when it comes time to begin our day, it doesn't appear to be unusual to open our email inbox, check our telephone, and search for our most recent walking orders.

I think this is an error. The errands relegated to us by others may appear to be critical, yet what is pressing is only here and there significant. The significant errands in our lives are the ones that move our expectations, our fantasies, our manifestations, and our organizations forward.

Does that imply that we ought to disregard our obligations as guardians or representatives or residents? Obviously not. However, we as a whole need an existence in our days to react to our own plan, not somebody else's.

Not a Morning Person?

Does the word morning cause you to grieve? Does the morning sun help you to remember The Eye of Sauron? Would you be able to consider nothing more regrettable than beams of brilliant daylight streaming delicately onto your pad?

No concerns, evening people.

As I examined the day by day propensities for several writers, craftsmen, and performers in Daily Rituals (book recording), I saw a significant pattern: There was no pattern.

There is nobody approach to be effective. There are similarly the same number of evening people delivering fantastic work as there are prompt risers. Be that as it may, regardless of what their specific routine resembled, each gainful craftsman grasped securing a holy time every day when they could deal with their own plan.

I discover morning to work best. Your mileage may shift.

The expression "Do the most significant thing first every day" is only a basic method of saying, "Give yourself a reality to chip away at what is imperative to you every day."

Instructions to Start Working Out When You Don't Know What You're Doing

What do you do when you're attempting to begin another exercise schedule?

Perhaps you've been preparing as long as you can remember and simply need another activity to keep things new. Or on the other hand possibly you're beginning with practice just because and don't have the foggiest idea how to begin working out. In any case, beginning another preparation routine is something we as a whole arrangement with occasionally.

For instance, I as of late added run preparing to my exercise schedule. There's only one issue: I've never done run preparing.

In this post, I'll diagram the systems I used to begin with another preparation routine and tell you the best way to begin working out.

Step by step instructions to Start Working Out

1.Decide what you need to be acceptable at doing.

I've expounded beforehand on how significant a feeling of direction can be, and that remains constant for exercise and preparing also.

The more explicit you are about what you need to turn out to be acceptable at doing, the simpler it is for you to prepare for progress. For my situation, I need to turn out to be acceptable at 400m runs. That is an unmistakable objective and it gives guidance to me simultaneously.

On the off chance that you're befuddled about how to begin turning out to be, at that point settle on a choice. It doesn't need to be the "best" choice. Simply pick something that you need to turn out to be acceptable at doing and begin moving toward that path. There will be a lot of time for modifications and improvement later.

2. Ask somebody who has been there.

Initially, I had no clue about what a normal run exercise even resembled.

How could I discover? I asked individuals who knew. Try not to be hesitant to connect and pose inquiries. Everyone is an apprentice sooner or later. The individuals around you are your most noteworthy resource.

I went to my quality and molding mentor from school, my old colleagues who had done run preparing, and a companion who ran track seriously. I approached every one of them for recommendations and projects for 400m run preparing and for general running tips.

My expectation was that by soliciting five distinct individuals rather from only one, I would get an all the more balanced view. True to form, everybody pointed me towards various projects and schedules.

While the entirety of this diverse data may appear to be clashing and confounding from the outset, it's significant for the subsequent stage.

3. Get the fundamental thought, avoid the subtleties.

This is the place a great many people surrender and never start their new daily schedule. (Try not to stress. It's transpired also.)

Wellness is one of the most noticeably awful businesses in case you're searching for clear guidance. It appears as though everybody has an alternate method of getting things done and they are totally persuaded that their way is the main way.

Therefore, it's anything but difficult to worry over the subtleties of another exercise schedule. Would it be advisable for me to do 5 sets or 6 sets? Program A says I should rest for 90 seconds, however Program B says I should rest for 60 seconds. This site says to exercise on Monday, Wednesday, Friday, however my companion did it on Tuesday and Thursday. Which one is correct?

We should all take a full breath.

Here's a little information bomb for you: the subtleties don't make a difference initially.

You'll have a lot of time to make sense of strategy, rest periods, volume, preparing plans, whatever blah. At the point when you're beginning another exercise schedule, the main thing that issues is beginning. Get the primary thought, adhere to the timetable, and the subtleties will start to become all-good.

Here's the means by which I did it with my run preparing…

I read every one of the assets and exercise programs that my companions sent me. At that point, I recorded the regular thoughts from each program.

This is what they resembled…

run runs that run from 200m to 500m

rest for 2 or 3 minutes between sets

run between 3 to 6 runs for each exercise

do run exercises 2 or 3 times each week

Did I forget about a ton of subtleties? Truly. However, with the fundamental thoughts above, I could go to the track and complete my first run exercise.

What's more, in the first place that is the genuine objective: make it as basic as conceivable to begin.

4. Go moderate.

More often than not, when we choose to begin another exercise schedule this is on the grounds that we're persuaded to do it. It's extraordinary to have inspiration, however as I've referenced previously, it very well may be a twofold edged blade.

Why? Initially, on the grounds that inspiration varies. This implies you can't depend on it. That is the reason you need to manufacture great propensities as opposed to getting inspired.

Yet, furthermore, inspiration can trick you into taking on more than you can realistically handle. (I expounded on why this is an issue, and how to dodge it, here.)

In the first place, you need to begin moderate. Keep in mind, the objective is to start doing the exercises, not to do extraordinary exercises.

Here's the way I began with my runs...

The main exercise, I completed 3 runs of 200m at half force. It was simple and moderate. I was just attempting to get my body used to running once more.

The subsequent exercise, I completed 2 runs of 400m with 3 minutes rest in the middle. Once more, this was certifiably not an especially burdening exercise.

Before all else, you need the exercises to be simple. This is valid for the initial 3 or a month. Your solitary objective is to adhere to the timetable and fabricate the ability to do the exercise. Execution doesn't make a difference.

It appears as though this is the specific inverse of what the vast majority do. The ordinary methodology is to go from sitting on your love seat to doing P90X for six days consistently. With a switch that way, it's no big surprise that a great many people surrender following seven days.

5. Try not to miss exercises.

In the event that I could sum up all that I've learned in 10 years of solidarity preparing it would come down to these three words: don't miss exercises.

In case we're being straightforward with ourselves, this is what our exercise schedule normally resembles:

Exercise reliably for a month or two.

Become ill. Miss various exercises. Spend the following month getting back fit as a fiddle.

Exercise reliably for a month or two.

Timetable changes. Life gets insane. Miss various exercises. Spend the following month getting back fit as a fiddle.

Exercise reliably for a month or two.

Travel. Excursion. Downtime. Miss different exercises. Spend the following month getting back fit as a fiddle.

Unendingly.

Presently there's nothing amiss with your timetable changing or taking get-away, yet you have to have a framework to make it as simple as conceivable to refocus. This is particularly evident when you're simply beginning with another exercise schedule.

At the point when I began my pushup schedule, I figured out how to get 17 successive exercises in before I missed a day. What's more, I got directly in the groove again after that one three day weekend. Altogether, I've done 93 pushup exercises in the course of the most recent 8 months.

The individual effect of every exercise has been little, however the aggregate effect of adhering to that timetable has been enormous. (I've multiplied the measure of pushups that I can do.) And everything comes down to not missing exercises.

I'm anticipating applying this equivalent system to my run exercises and I recommend you do likewise.

6. Pick an activity and begin

There are a larger number of activities on the planet than I want to check, yet I figure you can list the significant ones on two hands.

Quick lift

Grab

Squat

Deadlift

Seat Press

Pushups

Pullups

Runs

Pick one that you might want to be acceptable at and begin.

Keep in mind, you don't have to stress over the subtleties before all else. Simply get the principle thought, start moderate, and don't miss exercises.

Also, presently in the event that you'll pardon me, it's an ideal opportunity to hit the track.

Effective People Start Before They Feel Ready

In 1966, a dyslexic sixteen-year-old kid dropped out of school. With the assistance of a companion, he began a magazine for understudies and brought in cash by offering promotions to nearby organizations. With just a smidgen of cash to begin, he force the activity to leave the grave inside a neighborhood church.

After four years, he was searching for approaches to develop his little magazine and began selling mail request records to the understudies who purchased the magazine. The records sold alright that he fabricated his first record store the following year. Following two years of selling records, he chose to open his own record mark and recording studio.

He leased the account studio out to nearby specialists, including one named Mike Oldfield. In that little account studio, Oldfield made his hit melody, Tubular Bells, which turned into the record name's first delivery. The tune proceeded to sell more than 5 million duplicates.

Throughout the following decade, the little youngster developed his record name by including groups like the Sex Pistols, Culture Club, and the Rolling Stones. En route, he kept beginning organizations: a carrier business, at that point trains, at that point cell phones, without any end in sight. Just about 50 years after the fact, there were more than 400 organizations under his heading.

Today, that little youngster who dropped out of school and continued beginning things regardless of his naiveté and absence of information is an extremely rich person. His name is Sir Richard Branson.

How I Met Sir Richard Branson

Fourteen days prior, I strolled into a meeting room in Moscow, Russia and plunked down ten feet from Branson. There were 100 others around us, yet it seemed like we were having a discussion in my lounge. He was grinning and chuckling. His answers appeared to be unrehearsed and certified.

At a certain point, he recounted to the tale of how he began Virgin Airlines, a story that appears to catch his whole way to deal with business and life. Here's the variant he let us know, admirably well recall it:

"I was in my late twenties, so I had a business, yet no one knew who I was at that point. I was made a beeline for the Virgin Islands and I had a pretty young lady hanging tight for me, so I was, umm, resolved to arrive on schedule.

At the air terminal, my last trip to the Virgin Islands was dropped due to upkeep or something. It was the last trip out that night. I thought this was absurd, so I proceeded to sanction a private plane to take me to the Virgin Islands, which I didn't have the cash to do.

At that point, I got a little chalkboard, stated "Virgin Airlines. $29." on it, and headed toward the gathering of individuals who had been on the flight that was dropped. I sold tickets for the remainder of the seats on the plane, utilized their cash to pay for the sanctioned plane, and we as a whole went to the Virgin Islands that night."

— Richard Branson

I snapped this picture directly after he recounted to that story. A couple of seconds after the fact I stood side by side with him (he's around six feet tall) and expressed gratitude toward him for offering some an ideal opportunity to us.

The Habits of Successful People

Subsequent to talking with our gathering, Branson sat on a board with industry specialists to discuss the fate of business. As everybody around him was filling the air with business popular expressions and discussing complex thoughts for delineating our future, Branson was making statements like: "Screw it, simply jump on and do it." Which was firmly trailed by: "For what reason wouldn't we be able to mine space rocks?"

As I gazed toward that board, I understood that the individual who sounded the most oversimplified was likewise the one in particular who was an extremely rich person. Which incited me to ponder, "What's the contrast among Branson and every other person in the room?"

This is what I think has a significant effect:

Branson doesn't only make statements like, "Screw it, simply jump on and do it." He really carries on with his life that way. He drops out of school and starts a business. He signs the Sex Pistols to his record name when every other person says they are excessively questionable. He contracts a plane when he doesn't have the cash.

At the point when every other person shies away or concocts a valid justification for why the time isn't right, Branson begins. He makes sense of how to quit tarrying and venture out regardless of whether it appears to be abnormal.

Start Now

Branson is an outrageous model, however we could all take in something from his methodology.

On the off chance that you need to sum up the propensities for effective individuals into one expression, it's this: fruitful individuals start before they feel prepared.

On the off chance that there was ever somebody who exemplified beginning before they felt prepared to do as such, it's Branson. The very name of his business realm, Virgin, was picked in light of the fact that when Branson and his accomplices began they were "virgins" when it came to business.

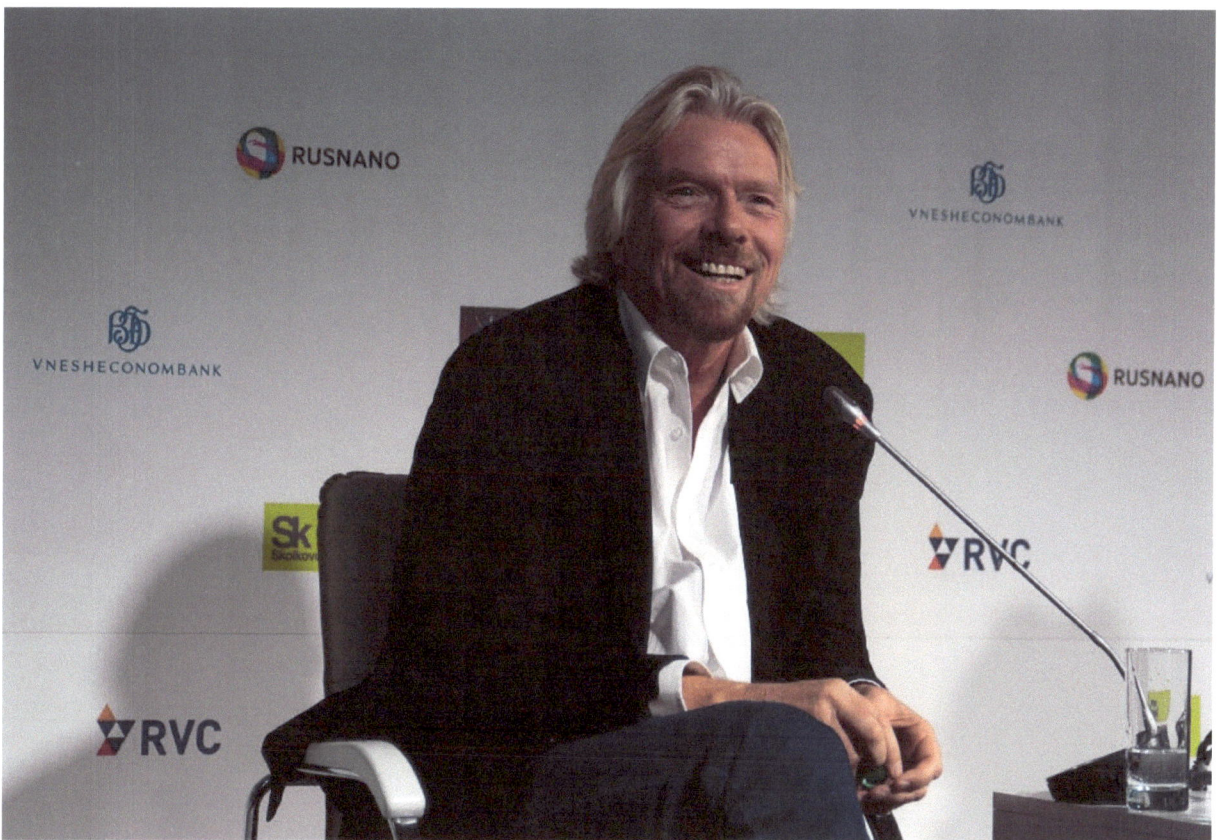

Branson has such a large number of numerous organizations, adventures, noble cause, and campaigns that it's just unrealistic for him to have felt arranged, qualified, and prepared to begin every one of them. Indeed, it's impossible that he was qualified or arranged to begin any of them. He had never flown a plane and knew nothing about the designing of planes, however he began an aircraft organization at any rate. He is an ideal case of why the "divinely selected individuals" pick themselves.

In the event that you're dealing with something significant, at that point you'll never feel prepared. A reaction of accomplishing testing work is that you're pulled by fervor and pushed by disarray simultaneously.

Will undoubtedly feel questionable, ill-equipped, and unfit. In any case, let me guarantee you of this: what you have right presently is sufficient. You can plan, postponement, and change all you need, yet trust me, what you have now is sufficient to begin. It doesn't make a difference in case you're attempting to begin a business, get thinner, compose a book, or accomplish quite a few objectives... what your identity is, the thing that you have, and what you realize right presently is sufficient to get moving.

We as a whole beginning in a similar spot: no cash, no assets, no contacts, no experience. The thing that matters is that a few people — the victors — decide to begin in any case.

Regardless of where you are on the planet and paying little mind to what you're dealing with, I trust you'll begin before you feel prepared.

The Magic of Committing to a Specific Goal

In our uproarious universe of performing various tasks, consistently associated, and overstimulated work, it's anything but difficult to live in a steady condition of interruption.

Yet, it doesn't need to be that way.

Recently, as I wrapped up a 5–roadtrip in San Francisco, I was helped to remember the intensity of investing in a solitary errand.

I woke up a couple of hours before dawn, passed through the obscurity and out of the city, climbed for 30 minutes to the head of a slope sitting above the Golden Gate Bridge, and snapped this photograph…

As I remained there absorbing the early morning light, I was helped to remember a significant exercise that is perilously not entirely obvious: on the off chance that you focus on an errand as opposed to contemplating a craving, you complete something.

The Dangerous Mistake We All Make

At the point when I showed up in San Francisco, I let myself know, "Simply take photographs as you do different things." My essential objective was to meet with companions thus I figured I could accept pictures as we strolled around the city. This brought about precisely zero photographs worth sharing.

I had obscure thoughts like, "I'd prefer to do some road photography," however I never went out with the purpose of capturing something explicit. At long last, on the last morning, I went out with the plan of catching a particular picture and I wound up with something worth sharing.

Book: The Ivy Lee Method The Daily Routine Experts Recommend for Peak Productivity
Author: Sikandar Sami

My misstep was that I expected that since I needed to take photographs, I would wind up getting an attractive outcome.

How regularly do you do this in your own life?

We ponder our unclear wants without focusing on a particular errand. We go to the rec center to "work out" without attempting to turn out to be better at something explicit. We need to "get more grounded" without considering the specific muscle bunches that we need to concentrate on. We wish that we were more innovative, yet never take a shot at a specific undertaking.

Clearness Leads to Direction

The entirety of the wide inquiries we pose to ourselves, similar to "What should I do with my life?" or "Will I ever discover love?" or "Is there importance to what I do?" ... none of those inquiries make it clear about what you ought to do straightaway.

At the point when you focus on an undertaking, nonetheless, at that point the following stage is self-evident. You need to snap a photo of the Golden Gate Bridge at dawn? Following stage: locate a decent spot. You've discovered a decent spot? Subsequent stage: get up right on time and drive there.

In the event that you just consider what you need, at that point you'll wind up mistook or baffled for luke warm outcomes, best case scenario.

Your decisions will become all-good on the off chance that you have a course to move towards.

Responsibility to playing out a particular undertaking is regularly the main distinction between our outcomes and our wants.

Start It Now

Book: The Ivy Lee Method The Daily Routine Experts Recommend for Peak Productivity
Author: Sikandar Sami

"Until one is submitted, there is aversion, the opportunity to step back. Concerning all demonstrations of activity (and creation), there is one basic truth, the obliviousness of which executes endless thoughts and wonderful plans: that the second one certainly submits oneself, at that point Providence moves as well. A wide range of things happen to help one that could never in any case have happened. An entire stream of occasions issues from the choice, bringing up in support of oneself all way of unanticipated occurrences and gatherings and material help, which no man could have envisioned would have come his direction. Whatever you can do, or dream you can do, start it. Intensity has virtuoso, force, and enchantment in it. Start it now."

— W.H. Murray

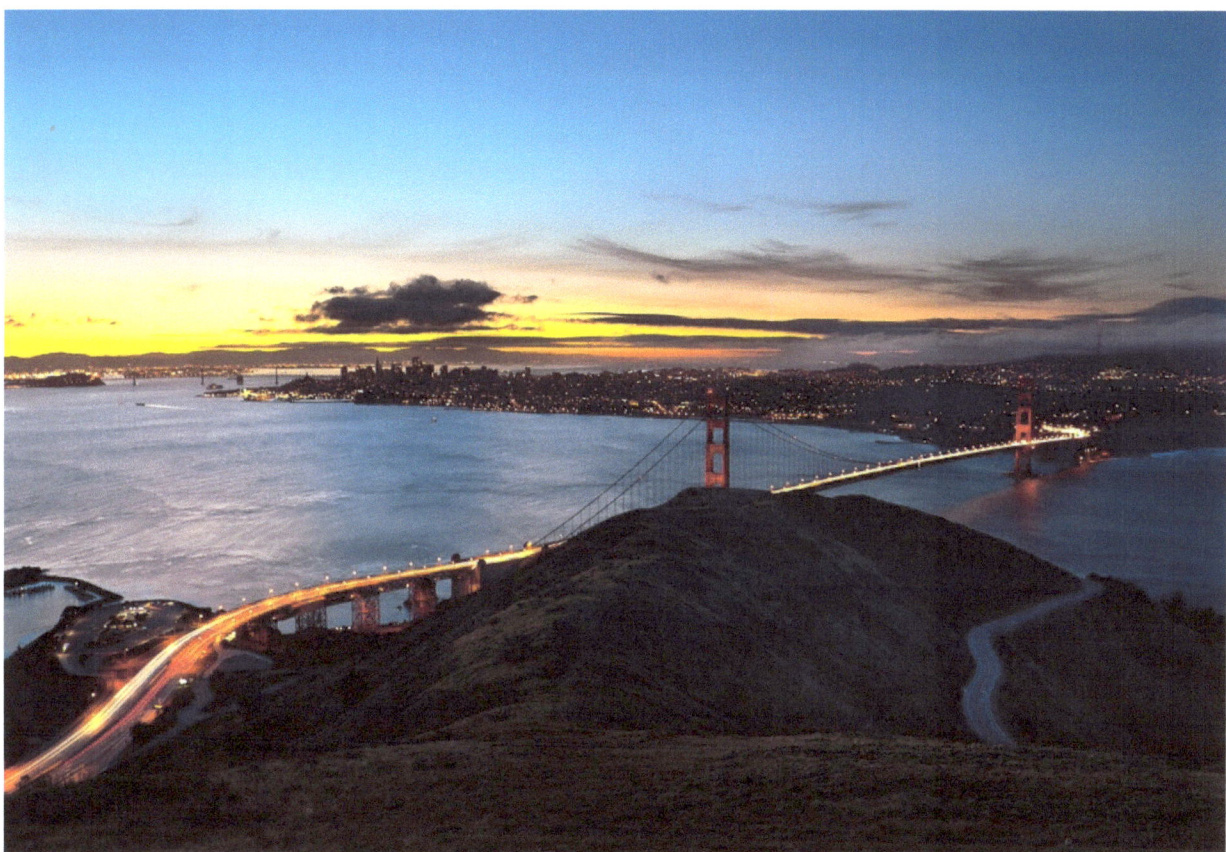

So frequently, we abstain from having a special interest in a particular objective out of dread that we pick an inappropriate one. Maybe we overlook that we can generally alter our choices later on.

This is maybe the most stunning thing about focusing on a particular objective: in the event that you confine yourself, at that point you'll start to break out and accomplish an option that could be more prominent than you at any point envisioned.

Book: The Ivy Lee Method The Daily Routine Experts Recommend for Peak Productivity
Author: Sikandar Sami

www.ingramcontent.com/pod-product-compliance
Lightning Source LLC
Chambersburg PA
CBHW051838210526
45473CB00005B/1933